Forty Days
and
FORTY NIGHTS!

Devotions For New Mothers

Michelle Waters

CSS Publishing Company, Inc., Lima, Ohio

FORTY DAYS AND FORTY NIGHTS!

Copyright © 2004 by
CSS Publishing Company, Inc.
Lima, Ohio

All scripture quotations unless marked otherwise are take from the *Holy Bible, New International Version*. Copyright © 1973, 1978, 1984 International Bible Society. Used by permission of Zondervan Bible Publishers. All rights reserved.

Scripture quotations marked (NRSV) are from the *New Revised Standard Version of the Bible*, copyright 1989 by the Division of Christian Education of the National Council of the Churches of Christ in the USA. Used by permission.

Scripture quotations marked (RSV) are from the *Revised Standard Version of the Bible*, copyrighted 1946, 1952 ©, 1971, 1973, by the Division of Christian Education of the National Council of the Churches of Christ in the USA. Used by permission.

Scripture quotations marked (The Message) are taken from *THE MESSAGE*. Copyright © by Eugene H. Peterson, 1992, 1994, 1995, 1996, 2000, 2001, 2002. Used by permission of NavPress Publishing Group.

For more information about CSS Publishing Company resources, visit our website at www.csspub.com or e-mail us at custserv@csspub.com or call (800) 241-4056.

ISBN 0-7880-2314-4

PRINTED IN U.S.A.

To
Sophia Grace

Preface

It rained for forty days and forty nights in Noah's day, the Israelites had to wander the wilderness for forty years, and Jesus was tempted by the devil for — you guessed it — forty days. See a pattern here?

For some reason, God likes the number forty. And generally speaking, when God throws out one of his forty-day engagements, we'd be wise to run for cover.

The first forty days of your baby's life can leave you wondering how you ever, in your wildest imagination, thought you were prepared for this thing called motherhood. The myriad of parenting books warned you about sleepless nights, constant feedings, colic, and everything in between — but they forgot to mention that you'd have to deal with those things at the same time as hormonal imbalances, clueless husbands, constant visitors, and the "baby blues."

In God's great wisdom, God always provides an ark, a shelter from the storm. For mothers, it's very often a few quiet moments alone with God — being refreshed by his Word and recharged by his Spirit.

Michelle Waters

"So they asked him, 'What miraculous sign then will you give that we may see it and believe you? What will you do?'"

— John 6:30

"Well? What did it say?" my husband asked nervously.

"It's positive," I said in disbelief. "I can't believe we're having a baby!"

It took a whole lot more than a home pregnancy test to convince me that there was actually a little baby growing inside me. First, there was the doctor's visit to confirm the test. Then the exhaustion that hits most women during the first trimester. I didn't even feel like drinking coffee — this alone should have been proof positive for a caffeine addict like me.

But it wasn't enough. It wasn't until I heard my baby's heartbeat for the first time that I was finally convinced.

Apparently, human nature has a built in denial mechanism to protect us from disappointment and hurt. People who met Jesus experienced this when he appeared too good to be true. Could he really have fed all those people with a few fish and loaves of bread? Could he really have healed all those who were sick? Could he really be the One we've been waiting for all this time?

Even though all the evidence pointed definitively to "Yes, he's the One!" they remained unconvinced. It wasn't enough to witness something amazing. Hearts had to be transformed because miracles alone don't fuel our faith. They may remind us of God's power, but if we relied only on miracles, we would always be seeking another one. Only when we feel the living beat of Jesus' heart within our own, do we recognize him as our Lord and Savior.

O God, we believe, but we ask you to help our unbelief. In a world that relies on external proof and scientific explanation, we often grope for words to explain the hope we have in you. Give us the words to speak so that we may clearly share your power with others. Amen.

"Do not exasperate your children; instead, bring them up in the training and instruction of the Lord." — *Ephesians 6:4*

"Perfect timing," I thought, as the most recent special edition of *Newsweek* caught my eye: "Your Child: Birth to Age Three." My baby was due any day, so I grabbed the magazine and proceeded through the checkout.

According to the editors, however, my timing wasn't perfect at all. Apparently I had already gravely endangered my unborn child's potential by not subjecting her to a daily dose of "stimulation and feedback." Would she ever recover from the negligence of not buying *Mozart for Babies* and *WombSong Serenades*?

Even before "brain building games" and toys designed "to produce the most synaptic responses" in infants, God knew that parents might get a little starry-eyed and crazy in their desire to raise future Ivy Leaguers. His advice seems simple enough: "Stop exasperating that poor child! A little training and instruction in my ways will go a long way." After all, Jesus grew "in wisdom and in stature" long before *Baby Mozart* CDs and foreign language flashcards.

God of all knowledge, you have placed within us a deep desire to see our children flourish and prosper. Sometimes we go too far, pushing them to exhaustion and burn out. Forgive us, Lord, when we mistakenly teach our children that worldly success is to be prized above all else. Instead, let us model the abundant life that is found in you alone — a life beyond what we could ever ask or imagine. Amen.

"For you created my inmost being; you knit me together in my mother's womb. I praise you because I am fearfully and wonderfully made; your works are wonderful, I know that full well."
— *Psalm 139:13-14*

"Hallelujah! It's a girl!" the doctor joyfully announced as I looked upon you for the first time. Hallelujah indeed. The day had finally arrived and we saw for ourselves just how wonderful are the works of God — the miracle of life.

The doctor let me hold you right away. Your little eyes were wide open and we stared at each other for awhile, neither of us knowing quite what to think of this new arrangement.

Everything happened so fast after that. The nurses looked you over and took you away. Your dad and grandpa had had enough of this hospital stuff and went to get something to eat. Men! I was all alone. I almost despaired at this utter abandonment. Then I remembered this might be my last quiet moment alone for the next eighteen years! Better enjoy it while it lasts ...

God of miracles, the awesome power of creation was revealed to me today with the birth of my daughter. Pain gives way to joy as you tenderly place this little one in my care. Help me to be the mother you have created me to be and teach me to trust that you will guide me in the amazing journey ahead. Amen.

" 'Abba, Father,' he said, 'everything is possible for you.' "
— Mark 14:36a

Naming a baby can be a daunting task. So much to think about. Will this name fit your child as a baby? Will she grow into it as an adult? Will my mother-in-law like it?

Certain names carry a lot of weight. Making a dinner reservation under the name Michael Jordan, for instance, gets you a much better table than one for Jan Mullins. Sharing a last name with a college president, gives you special status among other applicants. There is power in a name.

The Israelites were so aware of the power invoked by God's name — and its potential to be wrongly used — that they refused to speak the name of God out loud. Instead, they said, "Yahweh," which is the Hebrew letters for "I AM." It's like calling God by his initials. For the Israelites, God's name was too powerful to throw around in casual conversation.

Jesus teaches us to pray in a radical way. Not only should we call God "Father," we can call him "Abba," which means "Dad"! We can speak to the all-powerful God in such an intimate way because we are his children, not his subjects. Thank you for loving us so much, Dad!

God whose name is power, teach us how to pray with a sense of awe, even when we use everyday language to call on you. Forgive us when we use your name for our own purposes, seeking your presence only in times of crisis. Teach us to let thanks and praise flow naturally from our lips as we go about the day's business. Amen.

"Weeping may remain for a night, but rejoicing comes in the morning." — *Psalm 30:5b*

"Are you aware that it's completely normal to cry at the drop of a hat for the next few weeks?" The nurse looked up from her checklist when I failed to answer right away. We had been going over a long list of things "every mother needs to know before leaving the hospital." I had to initial each item — proof that the nurses had done their job in training me to be a competent parent.

"Yes, I've heard my hormones might be out of whack for a while ..." I said naively. She was trying to suppress a smile, apparently sensing I did not know what I was in for in the days to come.

After a few days at home, I smugly congratulated myself for not caving in to the "baby blues." Then it happened; out of nowhere came what my husband began (affectionately, of course) to call "The Meltdown." Like clockwork, every night — just as our well-wishing visitors were leaving and my husband was returning from work — it would come without warning. Tears streaming down my face for no reason whatsoever!

More than half of all new mothers experience some form of the baby blues. We're not going crazy — we just need a little while to adjust to this major life change. No one warned us that the cute, cuddly, constantly sleeping little package we took home from the hospital would soon wake up and demand every ounce of our attention and emotional storehouses. Okay, maybe a few people warned us, but we never actually believed them!

Thankfully, "this too shall pass." In the meantime, buy some more tissues and don't even try to explain to your well-meaning husband why you are blubbering again.

God of our joys and our sorrows, thank you for reminding me that I am not in control of the world. These unexplained tears help me to surrender anew each day to you. Thank you for turning my tears into joy. Help me to ask for help when I feel overwhelmed and wipe my tears away as only you can. Amen.

" 'I am the Lord's servant,' Mary answered. 'May it be to me as you have said.' " — *Luke 1:38*

Have you ever wondered why Mary said "yes" to the Holy Spirit's preposterous suggestion? Still a young girl, not yet married, she agrees to carry God's child in a culture where unwed mothers could be stoned to death.

When God comes knocking at the door, it's usually not to keep us in the comfort of our own living rooms. God wants us to step boldly in faith, to take a chance on him.

If we choose to stay put, preferring the ease of our well-established lifestyles, we say "no" to God and he can't use us. Life in God is not static — it's all about change. "For in him we live and move and have our being" (Acts 17:28). God wants to take us to another level; to change us from glory into glory. It's hard to get moving when we fail to open the door of our hearts and let God in.

God who gives courage, embolden us to follow you more closely. Enable us to take brave steps, trusting in your guidance. Calm the fears that forever keep us from taking up our crosses and being changed by life in you. Help us to say "yes" today. Amen.

"Honor your father and your mother, so that you may live long in the land the LORD your God is giving you."

— Exodus 20:12

"What kind of a marriage would your mother and his father have?" The pastor asked in our first premarital counseling session. "Excuse me?" We were definitely confused.

The pastor then preceded to give us way too much information on Family Systems Theory — making sure we both understood that the families we grew up in would play a big part in how we related to each other as husband and wife.

The question seemed funny at first, but he was certainly right about one thing: we bring all sorts of "issues" from our families into our marriages. Getting married isn't a one-way ticket out of your childhood home, however good or bad that may have been.

We would like to believe God is talking to our children in the fourth commandment; telling them to be good kids and not give us parents a hard time. But the gathered assembly that day at Mount Sinai was full of adults — God was certainly addressing them too. Honor your mom and dad, God says, *so that* you can live long and good lives in the land God gives. God knows a society that neglects its elders and prizes youth above all else is not good for anyone — the young or the old. We need to show love and respect for the elderly around us so that our children will do the same when it's their turn to care for us.

God of the old and the young, your Word says that gray hair is a crown of glory, yet we have failed to respect the elderly and to treat them with dignity. Forgive us, Lord, for valuing youth above the wisdom and grace of the aged. Teach us to care for all the generations, Lord, as you have cared for us. Amen.

"And if Christ has not been raised, our preaching is useless and so is your faith." — *1 Corinthians 15:14*

More school violence on the news. A phone call about a high school acquaintance's sudden death. Unpaid bills that will have to be put off — again.

To make matters worse, across the airwaves comes a discussion of Jesus' resurrection. The guest speaker is claiming you don't have to believe Jesus rose from the dead to be a Christian. Excuse me?

If Jesus didn't rise, this messy, often miserable world we live in is all there is. If Jesus didn't rise, our suffering is meaningless. If Jesus didn't rise, I'm stuck with myself the way I am, not the way God intended me to be.

Paul minces no words when he reminds us that *everything* hinges on the resurrection: "If only for this life we have hope in Christ, we are to be pitied more than all men" (1 Corinthians 15:19). Thank God the tomb was empty. Thank God Jesus defeated death. Thank God we are redeemed from hopelessness. Thank God we have eternal life!

Everlasting God, you conquered death once and for all and took away its sting. We still suffer the very real pain and loss when our loved ones die, but you promise that death is not the final word. Comfort us in our sadness and carry us — through the Cross — to the glory of the Resurrection. Amen.

"These commandments that I give you today are to be upon your hearts. Impress them on your children. Talk about them when you sit at home and when you walk along the road, when you lie down and when you get up." — *Deuteronomy 6:6-7*

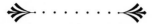

Considering there are over 600 laws in the Old Testament, it's no wonder God commanded the Israelites to talk about them all the time. How else would they ever remember all those seemingly obscure and random details — like only eating animals that have a "split hoof completely divided and that chews the cud" (Leviticus 11:3)?

Today, though, most families don't even find the time to have dinner together on a regular basis, let alone to discuss the finer points of God's law. At times it seems impossible to pass down our faith and values to our children.

Jesus certainly made it easier to remember the essence of the law — he gave us the *Cliff Notes* version: "Love the Lord your God with all your heart and with all your soul and with all your mind and with all your strength ... love your neighbor as yourself." Easier to remember for sure, but harder to accomplish! Jesus raised the bar, asking us not only to follow the rules but to change what's in our hearts. We can't just avoid bearing false witness (i.e. gossiping); we have to love the one we'd like to gossip about!

For Jesus, love is always about action. He loves by healing, by serving, by teaching, by dying. The only way we can instill love in our children's hearts is by our own loving actions toward others. Easy enough? Don't forget that includes loving the annoying coworker, the unfair boss, the angry teenager next door ...

O God, we love because you first loved us. You showed us the ultimate example of true love: that Jesus Christ laid down his life for us. You loved even the most "unlovable" of society. Help us to love all those who will cross our paths today so that they see a little bit of you in us. Amen.

"They said, 'Is this not Jesus, the son of Joseph, whose father and mother we know? How can he now say, "I came down from heaven?" ' "   *— John 6:42*

It's tempting to wonder sometimes how certain kids grow up to be Mother Teresa or Billy Graham, especially when we think their parents were just ordinary moms and dads like us. How could someone with so much godly influence be *her* son? How did *his* daughter change the world?

All moms and dads are just ordinary people doing the extraordinary work of raising God's children. When we let God enter into the equation, amazing things really can happen in the lives of our children.

The people who knew Jesus had a hard time believing he was God's Son because his parents were regular folks from a Podunk town called Nazareth. They failed to remember that no matter how mundane the circumstances of our lives may be, when God breaks into the world all things are possible.

Incarnate God, your own Son was born into circumstances we cannot even imagine. Through him we see your glory in the most unexpected ways: the lamb who is also the shepherd, the prince who is also the slave, the newborn who is also the king. Thank you God, for turning our expectations upside down and for showing us the mystery of your ways. Amen.

"Jesus looked at him and loved him." — **Mark 10:21a**

Everyone loves a baby. Regular errands take a lot longer with a baby in tow because people want to get a peek at your cute little bundle, offer some advice, or tell you about their own children. They'll praise your child's beautiful eyes or her perfect little button nose and act genuinely interested when you ramble on about your infant's most recent accomplishment. Babies are loved just because they're babies, not because of anything they've said or done.

The day will surely come, however, when that sweet little one will develop a mind of her own and find incomparable joy in testing the limits of your love. Most of us perfected this skill as adolescents. Loving us became more of a challenge for even the most patient of parents.

As hard as it may be to believe at times, God really does love us unconditionally. God knows everything we've ever done — even everything we've ever thought of doing — and yet God loves us nonetheless. We can't do anything to make God love us any less. Try as we might to test God's limits, God always welcomes us back with open arms. Why? Because we are God's children, created in his image, and held forever in his heart.

Loving God, you alone love us no matter what we do. Even in our most unlovable moments, you open wide your arms and make us feel like your favorite child. Help us to show our children how much we love them, even when it seems hard to do so. Amen.

" 'My God, my God, why have you forsaken me?' "
— Matthew 27:46b

I looked at my watch for the fiftieth time. Eight minutes. How can only eight minutes have passed? My pleading eyes met my husband's — "I'll go pick her up," I said.

"No, not yet," he said. "We'll do the check in two more minutes. You'll only make it worse if you go in there now."

Guilt-ridden, I put the pillow over my head. How can I let her cry like this? My little baby, all alone in her crib, was "learning how to fall asleep by herself." After ten days of getting no more than forty minutes of consecutive sleep, we decided our sweet angel needed to be able to fall back to sleep on her own when she woke up in the night.

Next to me were at least half a dozen books, opened to the pages that justified this insanity. "Letting your baby cry is harder on you than on the baby," or "Within three nights your baby will be going to bed quickly and easily by herself," or "Your baby will be much healthier and happier if she can develop independence in terms of her sleep habits."

My husband, calmly reading a non-parenting book next to me, was unfazed. I began plotting a way to sneak past him and rescue my baby. Just as I was about to make my break — silence. It was over; she was asleep.

"Tomorrow night," my husband said, "you go get some coffee; I'll take care of this." I was asleep before he finished his sentence.

Heavenly Father, loving so much makes me so vulnerable. Teach me how to set limits with love; to help my child grow and develop into the image-bearer you created her to be. Thank you, Lord, for the pain you suffered on our behalf, when you heard your own Son cry out to you on the Cross. Amen.

"But a true friend sticks closer than one's nearest kin."
                                    — Proverbs 18:24b (NRSV)

I was supposed to be concentrating on the man's lecture, but something about the slides really hit me that morning at church. Women in Tanzania flashed across the screen; pictures of such everyday rituals as bathing a baby or playing in the dirt with a young child.

What struck me was not their beautiful red *saris* or the elaborate, beaded jewelry around their necks. It was the fact that all these mothers were doing the daily tasks together.

In this country, mothering can be a lonely experience because we tend to do it behind closed doors. There are lots of stay-at-home-moms in my apartment building, but we only see each other as we're coming and going. We offer a quick, "Hi, how are you?" or "Your baby is getting so big!" before rushing back inside.

Jesus befriended the friendless of society: the poor, the sick, the suffering. He came so that even in our loneliest moments we might find friendship with God. He came to restore our relationship not only with God but with one another. What a friend we have in Jesus!

God of the friendless, thank you for seeking us out and befriending us. Teach us to do the same for others so that your love might be known everywhere. Give us the confidence to open our doors to our neighbors and to share the burdens and the joys of raising children. Amen.

"Cleanse me with hyssop, and I will be clean; wash me, and I will be whiter than snow." — *Psalm 51:7*

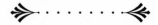

What did mothers do before Spray 'n Wash and disposable diapers? I'm constantly hosing things down with a stain removing cleanser and tossing them into the already heaping piles of laundry. Imagine adding cloth diapers to that load! A day doesn't go by without my daughter managing to soil both of our outfits at least once. Blankets, burp cloths, and onesies are perpetually soaking in my bathroom sink as I attempt to keep them looking good.

God is just as occupied with our inclination to mess up our lives. Fortunately, he took care of it once and for all on the Cross. We could never make ourselves clean enough to come into God's presence; only God can wash away our sin. But that doesn't mean we don't have to deal with the consequences of our actions every day. Nor does it mean we're let off the hook easily. We still have to give ourselves the daily once over, acknowledging the mess we've made and asking God to forgive us and help us clean it up.

Forgiving God, let me never forget to pray like David did: "Have mercy on me according to your unfailing love; according to your great compassion blot out my transgressions. Wash away all my iniquity and cleanse me from my sin" (Psalm 51:1-2). Amen.

"You will nurse and be carried on her arm and dandled on her knees. As a mother comforts her child, so I will comfort you...."
— *Isaiah 66:12b-13*

My head hit the pillow and my heavy eyelids fell shut. Sleep! In no time flat I would be in that much-coveted never-never land of new mothers. Or so I thought. My baby's rhythmic, heavy breathing had fooled me again; just when sleep was within my grasp, I heard that quick, snort-like sound that shattered my hopes of a little rest. In that one raspy breath I knew the sweet, sleeping angel at my side would cry out for food — AGAIN! Was I ever going to get some sleep?

Frustrated, I leaned my head over her bassinet and was immediately greeted with a full body smile. My groggy spirit was instantly uplifted. It's hard to be frustrated with a baby who's so obviously intoxicated by a parent's love.

No wonder God calls us to have the faith of a little child. My baby whole-heartedly trusts that when she is hungry, I will feed her; when she is sad, I will comfort her; and when she wants to "talk," I will be right there to coo and gurgle back at her.

God of all comfort, help me to depend on you just as fully as my baby depends on me. Let me rest assured that you are ready and waiting to meet my every need. Comfort me, Lord, as I comfort my baby, and refresh my spirit in the midst of this sleep-deprived state called motherhood. Amen.

"For in six days the LORD made the heavens and the earth, the sea, and all that is in them, but he rested on the seventh day. Therefore the LORD blessed the Sabbath day and made it holy."
— *Exodus 20:11*

"How are you?" a friend asked.

"Busy!" I said. "How are you doing?"

"Oh, it's crazy for me too! Not enough time in the day ..."

Before my baby was born, this was a normal conversation. Like everyone else I knew, I wore my busy-ness like a badge of honor, like it meant I was important.

With the baby comes a whole new load of responsibilities, but the pace is different. There are quiet moments of just holding her close, singing to her over the bathroom fan — her favorite "white noise." There are whispered prayers over her sleeping body and completely "unscheduled" times of playing on the floor and letting the afternoon roll by slowly. Best of all, there are those peaceful, middle of the night moments of nursing — just me and the baby — the rest of the world sound asleep.

That's the kind of time God desires us to spend with him. Losing ourselves in moments of worship. Freeing our schedules for time alone with him. Not constantly looking at our watches but being still and resting in God's love.

God of the Sabbath, thank you for the precious gift of time with you. Help us to step out of our harried schedules sometimes and sit quietly in your presence. Guide me to give my daughter time to dream, hope, and "do nothing," rather than filling up her time with as many activities as possible. Thank you for the refreshing rest we so desperately need. Amen.

"Pray without ceasing."   *— 1 Thessalonians 5:17 (NRSV)*

It doesn't take long to realize our babies are completely help-less little creatures. Without constant love, nurturing, and the pro-vision of food, warmth, and shelter, they cannot survive. And yet they have no words to tell us what they need and when. All they can do is cry out for our help. Our own prayer life is much the same. We come to God in a helpless state, needing him for our very existence. Sometimes we don't have the words to express the depth of sadness or the abun-dance of joy in our hearts. We cry out to God nonetheless.

A mother's heart is touched when she sees her child in need. A baby doesn't even have to cry and we are overcome with the de-sire to be there for her, to cuddle and protect her.

God's father-heart is touched even more when we reach out to him in prayer. God is busy satisfying all our needs, even when we don't take the time to express them in words. God does this de-spite our failure to recognize our dependence on him, or to take the time to thank him. Sound familiar?[1]

God of the helpless, thank you for providing everything we need, especially your love and protection. As mothers, you have given us a small glimpse of just how ready you are to meet our every need, to love and nurture your children with patience and tender-ness all our days. Thank you, Lord. Amen.

"Can a mother forget the baby at her breast and have no compassion on the child she has borne? Though she may forget, I will not forget you!"   — *Isaiah 49:15*

Our children's first understanding of God's character is linked to their image of Mom and Dad. Scary thought! If we are quick to forgive and merciful in our judgment, our children will learn that God is forgiving and merciful. If we are overly intimidating and harsh disciplinarians, they will most likely see God that way too.

Fortunately, God is not modeled after ordinary moms and dads. *We* need to model our behavior after *him*! Deep in the trenches of parenthood, even the best of us will make mistakes, feel inadequate, and sometimes even hurt those precious little ones we love so much. But God is the perfect parent — never forsaking us, always loving us, and tenderly disciplining us for our own good.

Father God, you know our shortcomings as mothers all too well. Thank you for loving us nonetheless. Remind us, Lord, that in spite of our failures, we are created in your image and you have blessed us and called us "good." Amen.

"Anyone who lives on milk, being still an infant, is not acquainted with the teaching about righteousness. But solid food is for the mature, who by constant use have trained themselves to distinguish good from evil." — Hebrews 5:13-14

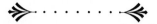

The much anticipated day had arrived: my daughter would experience her first solid food! I still don't understand how a little cereal mixed into a thick mushy substance is considered "solid," but that is beside the point. Having waited until she was truly ready (evidenced by the death grip she put on anything even closely resembling food), she managed to get most of the cereal down the first time around.

Overly excited about the feeding process, some friends began offering solids before their babies were ready. They certainly had fun videotaping the messy affair — food being flung far and wide from the little ones' mouths — but not much arrived in its rightful destination. After several frustrated attempts, these parents decided to wait a few weeks and try again.

Having a mind of their own, babies are quick to let you know if they don't want what you're offering. The same can be said about how we present the gospel message to those we love. If we give them too much too soon, the result can be a big mess. But if we slowly and tenderly plant the seed and trust God's guidance, we are much more likely to be fruitful.

God of all people, even in our busy lives as mothers you call us to witness to the truth of the gospel. Teach us how to share your love with others in our homes, places of work, and neighborhoods. Give us the words to speak and open up the door to conversation when the time is right. Amen.

"Then the man and his wife heard the sound of the LORD God as he was walking in the garden in the cool of the day, and they hid from the LORD God among the trees of the garden. But the LORD God called to the man, 'Where are you?' "

— Genesis 3:8-9

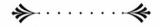

As I scrub crusty oatmeal off the side of my daughter's bowl, I daydream about a romantic night out with my husband. A restaurant that is not "family friendly," (i.e. they don't offer crayons and paper menus), dim lights, a bottle of wine ...

I remember some of our first dates, when the excitement was fresh and we had so much fun getting to know each other. I knew his class schedule and would go out of my way to cross his path at some point during the day. College! Surely we were meant to be together.

God may indeed have brought us together, but he has different ideas of what we are "meant for." We are meant to be in relationship with God. God knows us intimately and wants us to know him that way too. God seeks us out, never letting us get out of his sight, despite our best attempts to do so. God invites us on a "date" called prayer. No babysitters needed!

God, you search us out and know us like no one else does. You know our hearts and minds and yet you love us unconditionally. Thank you for inviting us into conversation with you, for calling us into relationship with the One who loves us, listens to us, strengthens us, and holds our hands through all the days of our lives. Amen.

"Immediately Jesus knew in his spirit that this was what they were thinking in their hearts, and he said to them, 'Why are you thinking these things?' "   — *Mark 2:8*

In my morning prayer time, I asked (all right, I begged) God to give me patience. It was only 11:00 a.m. and I was already frazzled. It took three tries to get my daughter down for her nap. The first time, she smiled up at me when I put her in the crib, as if to say, "Gotcha!" Then, on try number two, the cordless phone — conveniently left on her changing table — rang right as we walked into the nursery. Between tries two and three, I spilled what was to be my fourth cup of coffee. I was frustrated, irritable, and quietly seething.

Adding insult to injury, I remembered something I had read in a parenting book. Apparently, babies have an uncanny ability to be affected by their parent's mood. I was desperate to try anything so I took a deep breath and started over. Pretending to be serene and calm, I placed Sophie in her crib for the third time. Like magic, it worked! Not a peep came from the nursery this time.

Jesus isn't so easily fooled by outward appearances. He knows what is in our hearts, no matter how hard we try to hide it with false pretenses. But he also has pity on the paradox of human nature. We often do exactly what we wished we wouldn't: "When I want to do good, evil is right there with me" (Romans 7:21b). Only Jesus can rescue us from our sinful nature and give us true peace of mind.

God of peace, you bring order out of chaos and light out of darkness. Your peace is the only lasting peace we find. Yet it comes at a cost. The peace you offer was won through the suffering and death of your Son. Help us to remember that the daily struggles we face are so small in comparison to what you endured for us. Amen.

"Each one of you must also love his wife as he loves himself, and the wife must respect her husband." — *Ephesians 5:33*

"R-E-S-P-E-C-T ... find out what it means to me ..." Love and respect. Sounds easy enough. After all, why marry someone you don't respect? And most men would run from the altar if not for love. Where's the catch?

Obviously, Paul knew something about human nature many of us tend to forget: When the going gets tough, even the tough get going — that is, right out the door.

Lots of couples have unrealistic expectations about life with a baby. Seventy percent of new parents say they did not fully understand the incredible responsibility of parenthood or the impact it would have on their marriage.[2]

Sadly, 42 percent of divorces involving parents occur before their first child leaves kindergarten.[3] Maybe Paul's admonition to love and respect one another isn't as easy as it sounds. Just when we're at our weariest, when we feel the least like making the effort (diapers and spit up are not real romance boosters), God calls us to go the extra mile in our marriages.

God of love, help me to show my husband how much I love and respect him, even when I'm too tired to complete a sentence. Jesus loved the Church — his bride — by sacrificing himself for her and all the world. Teach husbands and wives to respect each other's hopes and dreams and learn to make sacrifices for the other. Amen.

" 'Come to me, all you who are weary and burdened and I will give you rest.' " — *Matthew 11:28*

Stretching out — and feeling strangely refreshed — I glanced over at the clock. 7:20 a.m. My husband stirred as well and our eyes locked. Did we just wake up on our own? Something must be wrong with the baby!

Eric dashed into the nursery, and came back with a less than satisfying report: "You've got to see this!" Peeking in, my wonderfully well-rested eyes beheld a beautiful sight. Sophie, fully awake, was playing by herself in the crib.

It's amazing how one full night of sleep can completely change your outlook. The day seemed brighter, my to-do list shorter, and the upstairs neighbors quieter!

Jesus promises that bringing our burdens to him in prayer is even better than those rare, uninterrupted nights of slumber. Resting in him refreshes and restores our sorrowing spirits in ways sleep never can.

God of rest, thank you for promising to carry all of my burdens. Help me to rest in you and to drink of the living water that truly refreshes my spirit. Amen.

"For the time will come when you will say, 'Blessed are the barren women: the wombs that never bore and the breasts that never nursed!' " — *Luke 23:29*

The insignia of my college flashed across the television set as the anchorman described the unbelievable: two professors, husband and wife, found stabbed to death in their small-town home. I remember the man; I took his course as a sophomore. I gasped and quickly flipped around to see if other stations had more information.

It would be days before the full story came out. Two teenagers from another small town had brutally killed the couple with weapons they bought over the Internet. Senseless teenage violence is all over the news these days, but this was the first time it had struck someone I knew personally. As I listened to the newscaster describe the events, I looked down at my daughter, asleep in my arms. What kind of a world will she inherit? How can I possibly keep her safe? Fear crept into my heart.

Jesus knows the anxiety a mother has for her children. He uses the mother-child relationship as the extreme example of vulnerability: when hardship comes, a mother may wish she never had children because of how excruciating it is to see a little one suffer. God intimately knows the deep-seated pain we experience in our troubled and turbulent world; he offered up his most beloved Son to a brutal death on our behalf. God alone provides comfort as he brings peace to a suffering and sinful world.

Suffering God, your presence is revealed even in the midst of our pain. Remind me, Lord, that no matter what happens in this world, you alone can free me from fear and give me the courage to love. Amen.

"He will yet fill your mouth with laughter and your lips with shouts of joy." — *Job 8:21*

After almost two months of constant feedings, messy diapers, sleep deprivation, and lots of tears (both baby's and mom's), something truly amazing happened. With glistening eyes, and arms outstretched, a smile at last spread across my daughter's face! This one tiny gesture is enough to convince you that all your self-sacrifice has been completely worthwhile. In fact, it's enough to make you totally forget all those sleepless nights and feelings of inadequacy. A short-term memory is truly one of God's greatest gifts to mothers!

A baby's smile has power beyond belief. Everything is fair game when you are trying to elicit that much-coveted smile. Mom and Dad are instantly reduced to blubbering idiots. Ordinarily stoic grandparents (you know, the Norwegian Lutheran type) turn into baby-talk peddlers right before your eyes — gurgling and cooing in a way you never dreamed possible. A surge of pride swells up every time you see that smile; surely your baby is this happy because of what a great mother you are!

How much happier is God, when he sees his own children taking pleasure in him, "Delight yourself in the LORD, and he will give you the desires of your heart" (Psalm 37:4).

God of all joy, thank you for my baby's smiles. Remind me today, Lord, that you are just as concerned with my happiness as I am with my child's. Help me to give all my cares to you, for you care for me like no other. Amen.

" 'Do not let your hearts be troubled and do not be afraid.' "
— John 14:27b

Sophie needs a hip ultrasound to test for dysfunction. Friends in the Red River Valley are sandbagging around the clock in an attempt to stem the tide of the cresting floodwaters. I attended two funerals last week: one for a victim of addiction, the other a suicide. Lord, how can my heart not be troubled and afraid?

Jesus doesn't ask us for false optimism. He doesn't even want us to see the world through rose-colored glasses. Instead, he comes to heal a world that he — more than anyone else — knows is broken.

Jesus steps right into our broken world and asks us to trust him. Trust that he is right there with us in the midst of our sadness. Trust that he will wipe away our tears. And most importantly, trust that one day there will be no more tears — only the joy of being in his presence for eternity.

God of the downcast and the weary, help us to trust you when our lives seem out of control. Remind us that you have a plan for us, even when all evidence seems to point to the contrary. Encourage us when we are down and lift our spirits when the world makes no sense at all. Comfort those who mourn and enable us to be a blessing to someone in need today. Amen.

"Train a child in the way he should go, and when he is old he will not turn from it."   *— Proverbs 22:6*

Susanna Wesley, the mother of those famous founders of the Methodist Church, Charles and John Wesley, took the religious education of her family very seriously. While her goal was simply "to take a more than ordinary care of the souls of my children ...,"[4] her method seems nothing short of a miracle to us harried modern moms: taking time every day to talk theology with each child alone (she had eight kids!), instructing them in the Bible, and leading the family devotions.

For most of us, this seems more than a little unattainable. Nevertheless, one hour on Sunday mornings is not enough for us or our children if we want to grow in relationship with the Lord.

The good news is that we don't have to be quite as regimented as Susanna Wesley to instill the Bible's teaching in our children. Bedtime prayers can easily be incorporated into the all-powerful "going to bed routine." Gardening can be a time to tell the many parables that deal with agriculture. Looking for a missing sock segues beautifully into the parable of the lost coin. These little things go a long way in teaching your child about God's presence in even the most mundane moments of our lives.

If you don't see immediate results, remember that God's timetable is different than ours. There's a reason God makes no promises for the faith of your teenager ... Instead, he assures you that "in his *old age*" your child will remember. Be patient!

Teacher God, give us the strength and wisdom to counter the culture's message of greed, violence, and instant gratification with your timeless ways of peace, patience, and putting others before ourselves. Teach us how to instruct our children in your ways and help us to lead by example. Amen.

"His delight is in the law of the LORD, and on his law he meditates day and night." — **Psalm 1:2**

The time has finally come. On top of my to-do list for the weekend, in bold letters, is: BABYPROOF HOUSE. My once immobile and easy to protect child is quickly learning to make her way across a room. Up to this point, we haven't worried about stray cords, exposed sockets, and all those crumbs, lost pencils, and who-knows-what-else hiding underneath our couches. With her new-found freedom, she no longer wants to be safely contained in the swing or bouncer. Soon we'll put up gates to ensure she can't wander away from the safety of the baby proof zones.

God's law functions in the same way. While God created us to be free — to choose how to live, where to work, who to love — he set up some boundaries so that we can do all these things without getting hurt. In fact, the law is intended to help us live joyful, fun lives.

Think of a hockey game with no referee. Can you imagine the mass chaos that would ensue? Sticks and elbows flying, needless punches thrown, checking from beyond — the game would end up in a brutish free-for-all. Without rules, we can't enjoy the game.

The game of life is no different. God doesn't want to see us hurt by unfaithful spouses so he tells us not to commit adultery. God would hate to have us waste precious time in jail, so he says don't kill or steal. God "adult proofs" our lives for our own good.

Giver of the law, thank you for showing us how to live with justice and honor. Forgive us when we fall short of your expectations. Thank you for sending Jesus to fulfill the law and to restore our broken relationship with you. Amen.

"Let us know, let us press on to know the LORD; his appearing is as sure as the dawn; he will come to us like the showers, like the spring rains that water the earth."   — *Hosea 6:3 (NRSV)*

It's raining AGAIN. April is almost half over and the sun has yet to shine. Yesterday it snowed! My baby and I are planning a silent revolt: we're declaring it pajama day and refusing to budge from the cozy comforts of home.

Sophie seems to enjoy the extra cuddle time and the carefree way we're going about the day. I think of the sad trend I heard recently: more and more kids are playing sick, not because they don't like school, but because they get to spend unstructured time with mom or dad. Despite our desire to have every moment of our kids' lives accounted for — soccer, piano, church, school — all they really want is some more time with parents. In other words, love is spelled T-I-M-E.[5]

Hopefully, tomorrow will bring some much needed sunshine. For now, I'm perfectly content to read *The Runaway Bunny* AGAIN, as we snuggle in our p.j.'s.

Lord God, let the rains renew the earth and your Spirit renew our souls. Let the first signs of spring remind us of the power of your resurrection. Amen.

"But I have calmed and quieted my soul, like a child quieted at its mother's breast; like a child that is quieted is my soul."

— Psalm 131:2 (RSV)

As I kneel at the communion rail, I think of Julian of Norwich, the thirteenth-century mystic, who compared the Lord's Supper to a mother nursing her child. Christ's body is given for me like I give my body to my daughter.

The pastor blesses us, "The body and blood of our Lord Jesus Christ strengthen you and keep you in his grace."

We file back to our seats and I feel the warmth of the strong wine settling in my stomach. It fills me up and reminds me of the power of God's presence. I sit quietly and thank God for this very special gift of himself.

I remember those first few weeks of Sophie's life, when I hadn't yet learned how to "read" her cries. My husband and I would exhaust every possible means of distraction, only to succumb to the one sure-fire solution: let her nurse *again.*

There were times when I questioned my decision to breastfeed. Resentment welled up as I felt I could never have a little time to myself or a full night of sleep. But now that we've got the hang of it — and she's adopted a much more manageable feeding schedule — I find the sacrifices more than worthwhile. This special time together restores both our souls as it nourishes her ever-growing body.

"Take and eat, this is my body given for you."

Sustaining God, you truly are the Bread of Life and the Cup of Salvation. Thank you for giving yourself completely to us: for feeding us, restoring us, and uplifting us with this spiritual food. Having been fed at your table, help us to become living sacrifices in Christ, to the glory of your Holy Name. Amen.

"The LORD bless you and keep you; the LORD make his face shine upon you and be gracious to you; the LORD turn his face toward you and give you peace."   *— Numbers 6:24-26*

While babies don't come with instructions, there are just enough parenting books out there to really confuse you. Lots of the advice in these books is completely contradictory. One simple tip, however, seems to be universal: you must have a bedtime routine!

Gone are the days of unscripted evenings, where dinner leisurely gives way to coffee and dessert or a television movie captivates your attention for hours on end. You are now a slave to THE ROUTINE.

We decided to go with a "B" theme: breastfeeding, bath, book, blessing, "Beautiful Savior," and finally, bed. Babies could care less what the routine actually consists of, as long as the essential ingredients stay the same night after night.

As my husband puts his hand on Sophie's head, he says the priestly blessing of Aaron. I never understood exactly what it meant for the Lord's face to shine upon me until I experienced the sheer joy my daughter exhibits when her dad looks down on her and blesses her like this. Remembering that God really does shine his face on us and look down on us with favor makes those long-forgotten quiet dinners and missed movies a little easier to do without!

God of all good things, thank you for blessing us tonight and for giving us the opportunity to be a blessing to our daughter. Give us all the joy of your face shining upon us and the comfort of a peaceful night of rest. Amen.

"May your father and mother be glad; may she who gave you birth rejoice!" — *Proverbs 23:25*

Martin Luther, a man quite fond of hyperbolic speech, held strong opinions about raising children. Preaching on marriage and the roles of mothers and fathers, he said, "Bringing up children properly is the shortest road to heaven."[6]

In true Luther fashion, however, he didn't let us off quite so easily or cheerfully. As always, the law is served up right alongside the gospel. Luther continued, "By the same token, hell is no more easily earned than with respect to one's own children."[7]

Knowing Luther's insistence on salvation by faith alone, we can be sure he didn't mean that our fate for eternity depends on how our children turn out. It relies not on what we do, but on what God has done for us.

His point is that our response to God's love for us is indeed important. God concerns himself with how we handle all the gifts he's given us — including our children. Luther reminds us "to regard children as nothing else but eternal treasures God commands us to protect.... "[8] Loving God means loving those little ones he's entrusted to our tender care.

Father of all children, Jesus welcomed the little children and held them tenderly in his arms. Forgive us when we, like the disciples, get in the way of our children's relationship with you. Help us to teach them of your love through our words as well as our actions. Amen.

"Therefore put on the full armor of God, so that when the day of evil comes, you may be able to stand your ground, and after you have done everything, to stand." — *Ephesians 6:13*

Putting a toy in Sophie's right hand, I grabbed the left arm and tried to sneak it through the sleeve of her shirt as quickly as possible. Having her arms in any way incapacitated — even momentarily — has become pure torture to this otherwise calm and sweet child. This time my ruse worked; the arm ended up inside the shirt and a changing table tantrum was averted. We weren't quite so lucky with the right arm, but one bout of screaming is better than two.

God wants nothing more than to clothe us in his righteousness — even when we kick and scream and try desperately to avoid God's tender pleas. We can't wear the armor of God because of anything we've done; it's all because of what God has done for us. We are made righteous — or in right relationship with God — because of Christ's death on the Cross. That's what grace is — God's **R**ighteousness **A**t **C**hrist's **E**xpense.

Sometimes the armor of God feels heavy and hard to wear. We want to squirm out of it and put on something more comfortable — something not quite so demanding. But nothing else ever fits quite right. Whatever looks more comfortable, or more convenient, ends up being a quick fix that doesn't last. Wearing God's armor may feel overbearing at times, but I wouldn't want to face the world without it.

Thank you, Lord, for clothing us with your righteousness, for giving us the weapons we need to stand firm in our faith: the belt of truth, the breastplate of righteousness, the shield of faith, the helmet of salvation, and the sword of the Spirit. Teach us, God, not to run from our fears but put our trust in you and the protective armor you've given us. Amen.

"For the LORD is righteous, he loves justice...." — *Psalm 11:7*

"It's not fair!" shouted one of the boys in play group. His little fists were clenched in open defiance of being asked to share the steel drum.

Children have no tolerance for even the slightest assault on what they believe to be "fair." This ranges from a three-year-old thinking she should be able to stay up as late as her nine-year-old brother to worrying about who got more whip cream on their piece of pie. Justice is a large-looming issue for kids.

God loves justice too. Fortunately for us, however, God's own system of justice is based on mercy — not fairness.

If God only cared about being fair, we would get what we deserve. We would be forever banished from the Garden, forced to live and die in the sinful world we created. But God is all about mercy. In his mercy, God allowed one man to pay the price for us all. With Jesus' death on the Cross, justice has been served. We are saved from fairness — we are saved from getting what we deserve!

This baffles adults as well as children. For adults, it's not God's justice that causes a problem; it's God's mercy. We don't understand how someone who makes a death-bed conversion can be given the exact same treatment as someone who has struggled her whole life to follow Christ. Isn't that just a little too much mercy?

God's ways are not for us to understand fully until we come face to face with him in eternity. Until then, we can sit back and trust that God's justice and his mercy are perfect, and they go hand in hand.

God of justice and mercy, you shower us with so many things we don't deserve: forgiveness of sins, relationship with you, and eternal life. Open our eyes to the injustice of this world, and give us ways to help those who suffer from its oppression. Guide us to be merciful, especially with our children. Amen.

" 'Why do you raise such questions in your hearts?' "
— Luke 5:22b (NRSV)

"Why doesn't your baby have shoes on?" little Jessie asked as I pushed Sophie in the swing next to hers.

"She doesn't need —"

"What is that?" she asked, pointing to the pacifier hanging from its clip on my daughter's shirt.

"That's her pac —" I tried to explain.

"Why...." The questions came fast and furious. I was completely caught off guard by a child actually old enough to talk, let alone the incessant questions of an inquisitive three-year-old. Trying to answer them all proved futile — Jessie preferred the search more than the find. She seemed completely unconcerned with my response — it was the question that mattered.

My own prayer life is often like that. I pepper God with questions until I'm worn out — sick of asking — and wondering why he doesn't respond. Of course I haven't even given God the chance. My own musings and concerns take center stage and I block out the wisdom God is trying to show me.

God certainly wants us to be like an inquisitive child — marveling at the wonder of his creation and wondering how his will is being fulfilled in our lives. But there are times when we overstep our bounds, when we feel entitled to know even the mind of God. He firmly, yet lovingly, reminds us — as he reminded Job — that there is a time to speak and a time to listen: "Who is this that darkens my counsel with words without knowledge? Brace yourself like a man; I will question *you*, and you shall answer *me*" (Job 38:2). Speak, Lord; I'm listening now.

Lord, you know our questions before they form on our lips. Thank you for curious minds and a desire to know more about you. Help us to listen more, especially in this culture where words are cheap and we are constantly overloaded with meaningless information. Even in our busy-ness, teach us to be still and know that you are God. Amen.

"Yet you brought me out of the womb; you made me trust in you even at my mother's breast. From birth I was cast upon you; from my mother's womb you have been my God."

— Psalm 22:9-10

Sophie's current toy of choice falls loudly to the floor. From her play station, she peers over the tray, looking for it. The toy remains out of sight — Sophie assumes it's gone and quickly moves on to something else.

Object permanence. That's the technical term for what she's learning now. Even though something is out of sight doesn't mean it's non-existent. Regular games of peek-a-boo help with this new lesson. Sophie waits expectantly while I hide my face; she's beginning to understand that it's not gone forever. The doctor says it's important to have her stay with a babysitter now and again as well, so she learns that Mom and Dad always come back after being away.

Our trust in God is modeled on the same lessons. We can't always feel God's presence — we don't see God in the room — but we know he's there. How? Because we trust. Why? Because God's proven himself faithful in the past. Even in our spiritual dry spells, we know God is with us because we've been through such times before and he's always made himself known to us again. God's absence is only our perception — it's not based on reality. As the old saying goes, "I believe in the sun, even when it doesn't shine."

Everlasting God, make yourself known to us in powerful and palpable ways today. Teach us to trust in your presence, even when it seems your face is turned from us. Thank you for never leaving us and help us to be just as steadfast and dependable to our children. Amen.

"Carry each other's burdens; and in this way you fulfill the law of Christ." — *Galatians 6:2*

Like parenting, serving in the name of Christ can be a thankless job. It can be painful too. I think of a friend who recently went on a short-term mission trip to Romania. Jenni volunteered in an orphanage — holding babies and talking to neglected children. The image of those little ones will never depart from her mind; so much pain already suffered at such a young age. She came back not only with a broken heart but with physical hurts as well: flea bites all over her body and a case of pink eye. These are the least of the problems suffered by the Romanian orphans.

We can't do this kind of service alone. It takes encouragement, support, and lots of prayers from our brothers and sisters in Christ. On our own, we might despair at the hopelessness of certain situations and throw in the towel. What can I really do to make a difference? It's only through the whole Christian church on earth that hearts and lives can be changed. We hold each other up in prayer, we give a helping hand physically and financially, we do the behind-the-scenes-work that makes some of the serving possible. Alone we are just a drop in the bucket. But together we see our efforts add up. And with God's hand involved, that bucket really does "runneth over."

God of the sick and suffering, you alone have the power to heal our hearts, minds, and spirits. Give us the courage and the resources to reach out to those in need, relying not on our own desire to do good, but on the awesome power of your Holy Spirit. Amen.

"God's blessing makes life rich; nothing we do can improve on God." — *Proverbs 10:22 (The Message)*

Changing diaper number ten, after feeding number eight, after reading book number six, I started to wonder when the adrenaline of new motherhood would wear off and the exhaustion would set in. I imagined my husband, coming home from work, finding me sprawled out on the living room floor, a puddle of drool on the carpet, and the baby wondering what happened to Mommy. There's no end to the work this little creature demands, day in and day out.

On good days, our apartment does not look like a tornado touched down — leaving debris of uneaten bread crusts, half-full coffee mugs, and bright colored baby toys in its wake. On bad ones, it's not hard to imagine the resulting disaster. I've completely squelched the desire to "straighten up" while the baby is napping. What's the point? It will return to a state of chaos as soon as she wakes anyway.

I'm constantly having to remind myself that when Sophie is grown and out of the house, I won't regret not spending more time cleaning. She'll only be a baby for so long — this particular blessing does not last forever. I'm surprised at how hard it is, though, to let things go unattended. There's always that nagging feeling, making me feel guilty about the state of disarray we live in.

God knows perfectly well how much we want to "work our way to the top." That's why God sent Jesus down to us. No amount of striving on our part would ever get us close to our heavenly Father. We may pride ourselves on our independence and ability to do things by ourselves, but that's not the way God's economy works. God knows we'd never find true peace if we had to rely on our own endeavors. God calls us to rely on him and the work he's done for us.

Lord God, your love is immeasurable, and yet we often feel that we don't quite measure up. Quiet our nagging minds and continually remind us what in life is truly important: relationship with you and with our loved ones. Thank you for the blessings no amount of work could provide. Amen.

I watched as the children walked up to the table, carefully inspected each glass of liquid, and wrote down their findings. The three clear glasses were filled with soda, all dark in color. The task at hand was to identify each type of soda without touching, tasting, or smelling. The kids could only use their eyes to determine what the mysterious beverages were.

The children's minister asked some of the kids to report their findings. They all guessed the obvious — that the glasses contained Coke, Pepsi, root beer, or maybe Dr Pepper. No one correctly identified which was which, though, so he called for a volunteer to do a taste test.

This proved simple for the soda-loving child who eagerly nominated himself for the job. "That's root beer," he said of the first glass. "Definitely Pepsi," for the second. "Oh, my favorite! That one's Dr Pepper!" Bingo, he got all three right.

The point is that using our eyes alone to experience the goodness of God is just not enough. "Taste and see...." We drink from the living water not only by seeing God's work in the world but by tasting the richness of the Lord's Supper, by touching the beauty of God's creation, by hearing the grace proclaimed in his Word. Living in Jesus is a sensory extravaganza!

Lord God, you provide the water of life and assure us that we will never be thirsty again. We continue to strive after the things that don't satisfy, hoping in vain that this time things will be different. Give us the courage to see, touch, taste, and hear of your goodness, so that we can be filled with the abundant life that you intend for us. Amen.

" 'For I know the plans I have for you,' declares the Lord, 'plans to prosper you and not to harm you, plans to give you hope and a future.' " — **Jeremiah 29:11**

The speaker at the end-of-the-year MOPS brunch had us all enthralled. It was the first time my daughter was left in the tender loving hands of the nursery volunteers. I relished the opportunity to listen with full attention and eat a meal without interruption. Imagine that!

Her message was about parenting with the big picture in mind. It's easy to get caught up in the minutia — sleepless nights, spilled milk, and runny noses — and forget that the ultimate goal is not to make it until bedtime, but to raise responsible, Christ-loving adults. She often imagines her girls in their wedding dresses — many years down the road — and hopes she's preparing them for the new roles and challenges that go along with leaving home.

God has always kept the big picture in mind. From the beginning of Creation, before Adam and Eve even looked at that tempting apple, God's plan of salvation in Christ was already figured out. His plan includes every single one of us. God alone gives us true hope and a future filled with blessings.

God of our hopes and dreams, you know our silent tears and our weary hearts, and yet you continually offer us renewed vision and strength in the plan you have for our lives. Make known your will to us today, as we try to raise our children to love and serve you. Amen.

Endnotes

1. O. Hallesby, *Prayer* (Augsburg: Minneapolis, 1931), p. 19.

2. Rhonda Kruse Nordin, *After the Baby: Making Sense of Marriage After Childbirth* (Taylor Trade Publishing: Dallas, 2000), p. xvi.

3. *Ibid.*, p. xv.

4. Sondra Higgins Matthaei, *Making Disciples: Faith Formation in the Wesley Tradition* (Abingdon Press: Nashville, 2000), p. 27.

5. Josh McDowell and Dick Day, *How to be a Hero to Your Kids* (Word Publishing: Dallas, 1991), p. 143.

6. Martin Luther, "A Sermon on the Estate of Marriage," in *Martin Luther's Basic Theological Writings*, edited by Timothy F. Lull (Fortress Press: Minneapolis, 1989), p. 635.

7. *Ibid.*, pp. 635-636.

8. *Ibid.*, p. 636.